TABLE OF CONTENTS

GUIDANCE

How to use these prompts for success.

Each category is a new step in your YouTube Career. These categories are designed to help you with every step of the process. From creating your channel to dealing with sponsorships, these prompts are here to guide you on your journey to YouTube growth and success.

Look at each one of these prompts as a tool in your tool bag. You could get the job done without them, but using them helps you speed up the process tenfold. It is important to think of each prompt, as its own formula as well. You have the ability to manipulate that formula in order to generate the perfect response for your situation. Feel free to ask your chatbot follow up questions that go along with these prompts. There is no set structure you NEED to follow. These are here to point you in the right direction and are the prompts I used in order to amass 4,000 subscribers in one month and start generating YouTube ad revenue within 26 days. I still use these prompts to manage sponsorship emails that are flooding in everyday.

I can't wait for you to grow on YouTube using These 53 ChatGPT prompts. Happy Prompting!

CHANNEL CREATION

1. Find your niche
2. Key settings
3. Channel name
4. Channel description
5. Profile picture
6. Banner image
7. Target audience
8. Channel tags
9. Homepage layout
10. Channel strategy
11. Brand identity

FIND YOUR NICHE

Formula

Find 10 niches based around [Topic of Interest], with good CPM's, and list 5 sub niches per niche that's listed.

Example

Find 10 niches based around Investing. with good CPM's, and list 5 sub niches per niche that's listed.

KEY SETTINGS

Formula

What are the key settings and features to configure for a YouTube channel based on [Your Niche]?

Example

What are the keyy settings and features to configure for a YouTube channel based on Investing?

CHANNEL NAME

Formula

Create [Number] unique, memorable, witty channel names for a YouTube channel dedicated to [Your Niche].

Example

Create 5 unique, memorable, witty channel names for a YouTube channel dedicated to Investing.

Channel Description

Formula

Create a YouTube channel description, with good SEO, under 750 characters, for a channel about [Your Niche].

Example

Create a YouTube channel description, with good SEO, under 750 characters, for a channel about Investing.

PROFILE PICTURE

Formula

What should I input within an AI art generator in order to generate the perfect profile picture for my YouTube channel based on [Your Niche], where my channel name is [Channel Name]?

Example

What should I input within an AI art generator in order to generate the perfect profile picture for my YouTube channel based on Investing, where my channel name is Cash Chronicles?

BANNER IMAGE

Formula

What should I input within an AI art generator in order to generate the perfect banner image for my YouTube channel based on [Your Niche], where my channel name is [Channel Name]?

Example

What should I input within an AI art generator in order to generate the perfect banner image for my YouTube channel based on Investing. where my channel name is Cash Chronicles?

TARGET AUDIENCE

Formula

Identify 10 aspects of my YouTube target audience where my YouTube channel is based on [Your Niche].

Example

Identify 10 aspects of my YouTube target audience where my YouTube channel is based on investing.

CHANNEL TAGS

Formula

Create a list of YouTube channel tags, with CSV format, with no quotations, that have good SEO for a YouTube channel based on [Your Niche].

Example

Create a list of YouTube channel tags, in CSV format, with no quotations, that have good SEO for a YouTube channel based on investing

HOMEPAGE LAYOUT

Formula

What are the best techniques for organizing my YouTube channel's homepage for good engagement for an audience geared towards [Your Niche]?

Example

What are the best techniques for organizing my YouTube channel's homepage for good engagement for an audience geared towards Investing?

CHANNEL STRATEGY

Formula

Develop a YouTube channel strategy and timeline to get [Number] subscribers within [Number] months with a channel dedicated to [Your Niche]. Make these actionable steps within the timeframe.

Example

Develop a YouTube channel strategy and timeline to get 2,000 subscribers within 5 months with a channel dedicated to Investing. Make these actionable steps within the timeframe.

BRAND INDENTITY

Formula

Create 5 unique selling propositions for my YouTube channel based on [Your Niche], in order to set my channel apart from the rest within the same niche.

Example

Create 5 unique selling propositions for my YouTube channel based on Investing, in order to set my channel apart from the rest within the same niche.

VIDEO CREATION

1. Video ideas.
2. Video length.
3. Video series.
4. Product reviewNS.
5. Q&A video.
6. Combine niches.
7. Product comparisons.
8. Niche myths.
9. Top 5 lists.
10. Niche skills.
11. Video scripts.
12. Engaging intros.
13. Witty hook.
14. Important niche subjects.
15. Videos for high CPM's.
16. Videos for subscriber gain.
17. Videos for engagement.

VIDEO IDEAS

Formula

Generate me [Number] YouTube video ideas for [Your Niche] to set me apart from the rest of the creators in this spaca.

Example

Generate me 10 YouTube video ideas for Investing in Cryptocurrency to set me apart
from the rest of the creators in this Space.

VIDEO LENGTH

Formula

What is a good length of a video based on [Your Topic], in order to maximize audience retention?

Example

What isa good length of a video based on Investing, in order to maximize audience retention?

VIDEO SERIES

Formula

Help me create a video series on [Your Niche] for beginners.

Example

Help me create a video series on Investing in Cryptocurrency for beginners.

PRODUCT REVIEWS

Formula

What are the top 10 [Your Niche] products to review in a YouTube video?

Example

What are the top 10 Investing products to review in a YouTube video?

Q&A VIDEO

Formula

What are some common questions people have about [Your Niche] that I can answer ina video?

Example

What are some common questions people have about Investing that I can answer in a video?

COMBINE NICHES

Formula

Help me brainstorm a video idea that combines [Your Niche] and [Another Niche].

Example

Help me brainstorm a video idea that combines Investing and Finance.

PRODUCT COMPARISON

Formula

Give me 3 video ideas where I compare [Product/Service A] and [Product/Service B] for my YouTube channel based on [Your Niche].

Example

Give me 3 video ideas where I compare TradingView and Thinkorswim for my YouTube channel based on Investing.

NICHE MYTHS

Formula

What are some [Your Niche] myths that I can debunk in a video?

Example

What are some Investing myths that I can debunk in a video?

TOP 5 LISTS

Formula

Give me video ideas for [Your Niche] top 5 lists.

Example

Give me video ideas for Investing top 5 lists.

NICHE SKILLS

Formula

Suggest a creative way to showcase my [Your Niche] skills in a YouTube video.

Example

Suggest a creative way to showcase my Investing skills in a YouTube video.

VIDEO SCRIPTS

Formula

Create a [Length] minute long YouTube video script, for a video that is about [Your Topic].

Example

Create a 5 minute long YouTube video script, for a video that is about Investing for Beginners: 4 Tips When Starting to Invest.

ENGAGING INTRO

Formula

Create an engaging intro script for a YouTube video that is about [Your Topic].

Example

Create an engaging intro script for a YouTube video that is about How to Invest for Beginners.

WITTY HOOK

Formula

Write a witty hook statement for a YouTube video based on [Your Topic].

Example

Write a witty hook statement for a YouTube video based on Investing for Beginners.

IMPORTANT NICHE SUBECTS

Formula

Create a list of the 10 most important subjects in a YouTube video that will resonate well to an audience of a You Tube channel based on [Your Niche].

Example

Create a list of the 10 most important subjects in a YouTube video that will resonate well to an audience of a YouTube channel based on Investing and Finance.

VIDEOS FOR HIGH CPM

Formula

Create [Number] YouTube video ideas about [Your Niche]. Find the video ideas that will generate the best CPM's.

Example

Create 5 YouTube video ideas about Investing. Find the video ideas that will generate the best CPM's.

VIDEOS FOR SUBSCRIBER GAIN

Formula

Create [Number] YouTube video ideas about [Your Niche]. Create video ideas that will make.viewers subconsciously want to.hit the subscribe button during the video.

Example

Create 5 YouTube video ideas about Investing. Create video ideas that will make viewers subconsciously want to hit the subscribe button during the video.

VIDEOS FOR ENGAGEMENT

Formula

Create [Number] YouTube video ideas about [Your Niche]. Find video ideas that make the viewers more apt to like and comment.

Example

Create 10 YouTube video ideas about Investing. Find video ideas that make the viewers more apt to like and commnent.

VIDEO OPTIMIZATION

1. Keyword research..
2. Video titles.
3. Video descriptions.
4. Video tags..
5. Thumbnail guide.
6. End screen set-up

KEYWORD RESEARCH

Formula

Help me find the most effective keywords for my YouTube.video on [Topic].

Example

Help me find the most effective keywords for my YouTube video on Investing for Beginners.

VIDEO TITLES

Formula

Suggest the [Number] best titles for my video about [Topic] to improve its discoverability on YouTube.

Example

Suggest the 5 best titles for my video about Investing for Beginners to improve its discoverability on YouTube.

VIDEO DESCRIPTION

Formula

Provide an engaging and SEO-friendly description for mny YouTube video on [Topic].

Example

Provide an engaging and SEO-friendly description for my YouTube video on Investing for Beginners.

VIDEO TAGS

Formula

Recommend YouTube video tags, in CSV format, with no quotations, for my YouTube video about [Topic] to boost its visibility.

Example

Recommend YouTube video tags, in CSV format, with no quotations, for my YouTube video about Investing for Beginners to boost its visibility.

THUMBNAIL GUIDE

Formula

Guide me in creating an eye-catching thumbnail for my YouTube video on [Topic] using [Software].

Example

Guide me in creating an eye-catching thumbnail for my YouTube video on Investing for Beginners using Photoshop.

END SCREEN SET-UP

Formula

Assist me in setting up an effective end screen for my YouTube video on [Topic] to increase watch time and promote other videos.

Example

Assist me in setting up an effective end screen for my YouTube video on Investing for Beginners to increase watch time and promote other videos.

MONETIZATION AND GROWTH

1. Monetization timefranme.
2. Improve CTR.
3. YouTube ads.
4. Posting schedule.
5. YouTube premium revenue
6. Revenue diversification.
7. Super chat.

MONETIZATION TIMEFRAME

Formula

What is the best strategy to monetize my YouTube channel, based on its niche, which is [Niche]. within [Timeframe]?

Example

What is the best strategy to monetize my YouTube channel, based on its niche, which is Investing, within 6 months?

IMPROVE CTR

Formula

How can I increase the click-through rate of my YouTube thumbnails for my channel in the niche, [Niche], in order to boost growth and monetization?

Example

How can I increase the click-through rate of ny YouTube thumbnails for my channel in the niche, Investing, in order to boost growth and monetization?

YOUTUBE ADS

Formula

What are the best practices for creating YouTube ads that drive revenue and growth for my channel in this niche: [Niche].

Example

What are the best practices for creating YouTube ads that drive revenue and growth for my channel in this niche: Investing.

POSTING SCHEDULE

Formula

Develop a posting schedule for my YouTube videos where I want to upload [Number] videos per week with my first upload being on [MM/DD/YYY].

Example

Develop a posting schedule for my YouTube videos where I want to upload 2 videos per week with my first upload being on 05/10/2023.

YOUTUBE PREMIUM REVENUE

Formula

How can I best utilize YouTube Premium revenue for my YouTube channel in this niche: [Niche]?

Example

How can I best utilize YouTube Premium revenue for my YouTube channel in this niche: Investing?

REVENUE DIVERSIFICATION

Formula

What are the most effective ways to diversify my YouTube channel, that's based on [Main Channel Focus]. for incomne streams beyond YouTube ad revenue?

Example

What are the most effective ways to diversify my YouTube channel, that's based on Investing and Finance, for income streams beyond YouTube ad revenue?

SUPER CHAT

Formula

Create a guide on howl can fully take advantage of Super Chat donations for my YouTube channel that's based on: [Niche].

Example

Create a guide on how l can fully take advantage of Super Chat donations for my YouTube channel that's based on: Investing.

COMMUNITY MANAGEMENT

1. Comment response.
2. Email response.
3. Engaging the community.
4. Interactive polls.
5. Contest ideas.
6. Social media posts.

COMMENT RESPONSE

Formula

Respond to this comment in a [Tone] manner: [Comment]

Example

Respond to this comment in a friendly manner: Hey, great information provided in the video, my only gripe is, you need to get better camera quality.

EMAIL RESPONSE

Formula

Respond to this email in a [Tone] manner: [Email]

Example

Respond to this email in a professional manner: Hey I love your videos! I make videos in the same niche, and I was wondering if you'd be interested in collaborating on a video together?

ENGAGING THE COMMUNITY

Formula

Generate [Number] steps in order to foster an engaged community in this niche: [Niche].

Example

Generate 10 steps in order to foster an engaged community in this niche: Investing.

INTERACTIVE POLLS

Formula

Create [Number] interactive polls for my YouTube communlty based on [Topic/NicheVideo]

Example

Create5 interactive polls for my YouTube community based on a video titled: Investing for Beginners: 4 Investing Tips.

CONTEST IDEAS

Formula

Organize [Number] contest ideas for my YouTube audience. My channel is based on [Niche]. Make these contests benefictal for my channel and the aucience.

Example

Organize 3 contest ideas for my YouTube audience. My channel is based on Investing. Make these contests beneficial for my channel and the audience.

SOCIAL MEDIA POSTS

Formula

Create a social media post for [Your Social Media of Choice] about my new YouTube video: [Video Title].

Example

Create a social media post for Twitter about my new YouTube video: Investing for Beginners: 4 Investing Tips to Get Started.

SPONSORSHIP MANAGEMENT

1. Sponsorship research.
2. Analytic tracking.
3. Negotiation.
4. Pricing strategy.
5. Alternate opportunities.
6. Red flags.

SPONSORSHIP RESEARCH

Formula

How can I find potential sponsors for my YouTube channel? Please provide a list of [Number] suggestions tailored to mny niche: [Your Niche].

Example

How can I find potential sponsors for my YouTube channel? Please provide a list of 10 suggestions tailored to my niche: Investing.

ANALYTIC TRACKING

Formula

How can I track the performance of my YouTube channel's sponsored content? Provide a list of [Number] tools or methods that I can use.

Example

How can I track the performance of my YouTube channel's sponsored content? Provide a list of 10 tools or mnethods that I can use.

NEGOTIATION

Formula

Provide a guide for negotiating YouTube sponsorship deals within the [Your Niche] niche. I want to ensure I'm getting a fair deal for both myself and the sponsor.

Example

Provide a guide for negotiating YouTube sponsorship deals within the Investing niche. I want to ensure I'm getting a fair deal for both myself and the sponsor.

PRICING STRATEGY

Formula

Help me create a pricing strategy for my YouTube channel, [Channel Name]. This channel is based on specifically on [Your Niche]. Please provide a list of factors to consider and a suggested pricing range based on my channel's subscíber count which is [Subscriber Count] and views month which is [Views Per Month].

Example

Help me create a pricing strategy for my YouTube channel, Al Wealth. This channel is based on specifically on Artificial Intelligence. Please provide a list of factors to consider and a suggested pricing range based on my channel's subscriber count which is 8,500 and views per month which is 150,000.

ALTERNATE OPPORTUNITIES

Formula

I want to diversify my sponsorship opportunities on my YouTube channel, [Channel Name], This channel is based on specifically on [Your Niche]. Provide a list of [Number] alternative revenue streams to explore?

Example

I want to diversify my sponsorship opportunities on my YouTube channel, Al Wealth. This channel is based on specifically on Artificial Intelligence. Provide a list of 5 alternative revenue streams to explore?

RED FLAGS

Formula

What are the most common red flags when considering YouTube sponsorship deals for a channel in the [Your Niche] niche. Please provide a list of warning signs to watch out for.

Example

What are the most common red flags when considering YouTube sponsorship deals for a channel in the Artificial Intelligence niche. Please provide a list of warning signs to watch out for.

The End

Thank you for your interest

www.ingramcontent.com/pod-product-compliance
Lightning Source LLC
LaVergne TN
LVHW081804050326
832903LV00027B/2096